IT'S COOL TO
LEARN ABOUT
COUNTRIES

Social Studies
Explorer

TURKEY

•—• by Vicky Franchino

CHERRY LAKE PUBLISHING • ANN ARBOR, MICHIGAN

Published in the United States of America
by Cherry Lake Publishing
Ann Arbor, Michigan
www.cherrylakepublishing.com

Content Adviser: Sinan Ciddi, PhD, Executive Director of the Insititute of Turkish Studies, Georgetown University

Book design and production: The Design Lab

Photo credits: Cover, ©David Berry/Shutterstock, Inc.; cover (stamp), ©AlexanderZam/ Shutterstock, Inc.; page 4, ©Dr Saqib-ul-Hasan/Shutterstock, Inc.; page 5, ©Sailorr/ Shutterstock, Inc.; pages 7, 21, and 34, ©ASSOCIATED PRESS; page 8, ©Clara/Shutterstock, Inc.; page 9, ©Images & Stories/Alamy; page 11, ©Peter Horree/Alamy; page 12, ©Pegaz/ Alamy; page 14, ©Brigida Soriano/Shutterstock, Inc.; page 15, ©Ancient Art & Architecture Collection Ltd/Alamy; pages 16 and 38, ©Michele Burgess/Alamy; page 17, ©North Wind Picture Archives/Alamy; page 18, ©DIZ Muenchen GmbH, Sueddeutsche Zeitung Photo/ Alamy; page 19, ©Keystone Pictures USA/Alamy; page 23, ©Viorel Dudau/Dreamstime. com; page 26, ©Ray Roberts/Alamy; page 27, ©Bart Pro/Alamy; page 29, ©Janine Wiedel Photolibrary/Alamy; pages 30 and 39, ©Vehbi Koca/Alamy; page 31, ©Stan Gamester/ Alamy; page 32, ©Stan Gamester/Alamy; page 33, ©Yuri Arcurs/Dreamstime.com; page 41, ©Ran Z/Shutterstock, Inc.; page 42, ©jabiru/Shutterstock, Inc.

Library of Congress Cataloging-in-Publication Data

Franchino, Vicky.
    Turkey / by Vicky Franchino.
        p. cm.— (Social studies explorer) (It's cool to learn about countries)
    Includes bibliographical references and index.
    ISBN 978-1-61080-442-4 (lib. bdg.) — ISBN 978-1-61080-529-2 (e-book) —
ISBN 978-1-61080-616-9 (pbk.)
1. Turkey—Juvenile literature. I. Title.
    DR417.4.F73 2012
    956.1—dc23   2012001717

Cherry Lake Publishing would like to acknowledge the work of The Partnership for
21st Century Skills. Please visit www.21stcenturyskills.org for more information.

Printed in the United States of America
Corporate Graphics Inc.

July 2012
CLFA11

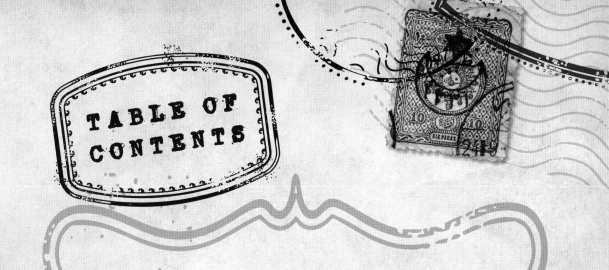

TABLE OF CONTENTS

CHAPTER ONE

WELCOME TO TURKEY!

➥ Turkey is home to many beautiful mosques.

Halfway around the globe lies a country split between two continents. Centuries-old **mosques** sit in the shadows of towering skyscrapers. Some families call a fabric tent home, while others live in apartment buildings. That country is Turkey!

Turkey's total area is 303,224 square miles (785,347 square kilometers). This is roughly the size of Texas. The area crosses into two continents: Europe and Asia. The European section of Turkey is called Thrace. Thrace is very small but does include part of Turkey's most populated city, Istanbul. Of the 73 million people living in Turkey, more than 12.5 million live in Istanbul.

↔ Istanbul is a major center of culture and trade in Turkey.

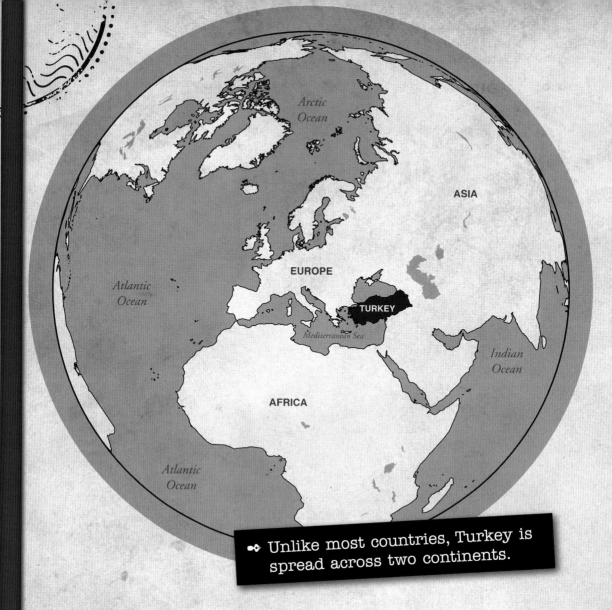

Arctic
Ocean

ASIA

EUROPE

Atlantic
Ocean

TURKEY

Mediterranean Sea

Indian
Ocean

AFRICA

Atlantic
Ocean

◦◦ Unlike most countries, Turkey is
spread across two continents.

Most of Turkey, including part of Istanbul, is on
the continent of Asia. This area is known as Anatolia.
Ankara, the capital of Turkey, is in Anatolia.

Turkey is a land of great contrasts. It is surrounded
on three sides by large bodies of water: the Black Sea,
the Aegean Sea, and the Mediterranean Sea. But it also
has areas that get little rain and are virtually deserts.

Western Anatolia has flat areas, mild temperatures, and **fertile** farmlands. Head east and the land begins to change. Here you'll find the highest point in Turkey, Mount Ararat. This inactive volcano is 16,945 feet (5,165 meters) tall. The region is also home to the Taurus Mountains, the source of two of Asia's largest rivers, the Tigris and the Euphrates.

Turkey has many earthquakes. Most of them occur along the North Anatolian **Fault**, which runs across the northern part of the country. Between 1939 and 1999, 11 major earthquakes happened in this area. The most serious recent earthquake was near the city of Izmit in 1999. More than 17,000 people died because buildings in the area were not designed to withstand earthquakes. Turkey also had many strong earthquakes in 2011.

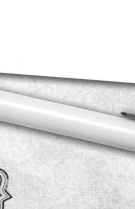

Pamukkale, or "cotton palace," looks as if it belongs in a fairy tale. It is a combination of hot springs, water-filled **terraces**, and "frozen" waterfalls made of a mineral called travertine. Today, Pamukkale is a protected national park. In the past, some people believed the waters at Pamukkale had healing powers. Other people thought it was a place of evil, possibly because it doesn't smell very good!

Travel throughout the country and you'll see both familiar and exotic animals. Wild cats, wolves, bears, deer, and geese are common. On the coast, you might see seals, dolphins, and turtles. Turkey is along the migration route for many birds. In fact, so many birds stop at Lake Manyas in northwestern Turkey that the lake's nickname is Bird Lake!

At lower elevations, Turkey has a variety of **deciduous** trees. These include alder, oak, and sycamore, as well as laurel, holly, and myrtle bushes. Climb into the mountains and you'll find **coniferous** forests. Many beautiful flowers also grow throughout Turkey.

❧ The mountains of Turkey are home to a wide variety of trees.

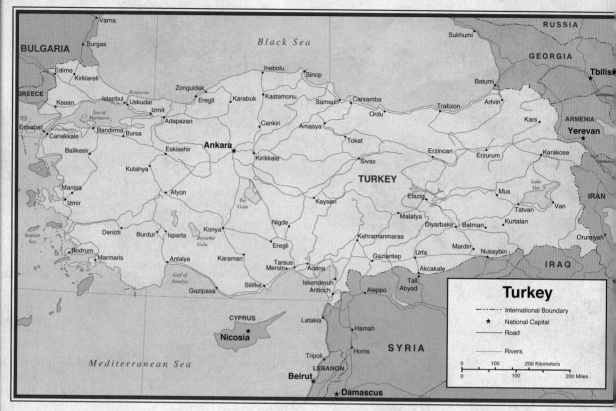

Turkey has its foot in two continents. Which of the countries surrounding Turkey on this map are considered European? Which are Asian? See if you can find Turkey's capital, Ankara, and its biggest city, Istanbul. Turkey's location makes it important for trade. If people are traveling over land, Turkey is a bridge between Europe and Asia. If they are traveling by water, Turkey has many seaports. Which Turkish cities on the map are likely to have ports?

CHAPTER TWO

BUSINESS AND GOVERNMENT

⚬ Mint leaves are just one of the many crops grown by Turkish farmers.

For most of its history, Turkey has been a country of farmers. The mild climate makes it a perfect place to grow citrus fruits, sugar beets, grain, cotton, tobacco, hazelnuts, and other crops.

◆ Many Turkish people earn a living manufacturing goods such as carpets and rugs.

Today, only about a third of the people make a living from farming. About one-quarter of the population works in manufacturing. Turkey has long been known for its **textiles**, but it also makes automotive parts, cars, electronics, lumber, and paper. The rest of Turkey's people work in the service industry. Lawyers, doctors, teachers, and people who work in restaurants are all service workers. In Turkey, tourism is a very important service industry.

Turkey has long been a valued trade route between the East and the West. As a result, many countries have conquered it—or tried to.

IMPORT EXPORT

You can learn about Turkey's economy by looking at its trading partners. Trading partners import, or buy, goods from each other. They also export, or sell, goods to each other. Below are two graphs showing Turkey's main import and export trading partners. Which countries are on both graphs? Does Turkey import more of its goods from certain countries or export more to others?

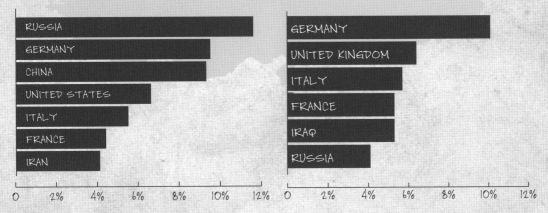

IMPORTS ⟶ TURKEY ⟶ EXPORTS

IMPORTS		EXPORTS	
RUSSIA		GERMANY	
GERMANY		UNITED KINGDOM	
CHINA		ITALY	
UNITED STATES		FRANCE	
ITALY		IRAQ	
FRANCE		RUSSIA	
IRAN			

0 2% 4% 6% 8% 10% 12%   0 2% 4% 6% 8% 10% 12%

A group called the Hittites took control of Asia Minor, in present-day Turkey, around 2000 BCE. The Hittite Empire continued for roughly 1,000 years. A series of groups then invaded Anatolia, including the Greeks under Alexander the Great in 334 BCE.

The Roman Empire conquered the region about 300 years later. Byzantium, present-day Istanbul, became the eastern center of the Roman Empire. The region became known as the Byzantine Empire.

➥ Greek warriors led by Alexander the Great invaded parts of present-day Turkey in 334 BCE.

➥ Byzantium went through tremendous changes under the leadership of Emperor Constantine and the Roman Empire.

In 330 CE, Roman emperor Constantine renamed Byzantium. He called it Constantinople. He also declared Christianity to be the official religion of the Roman Empire. Not long after, the empire split in two. One section had its capital in Rome. The other section, the Byzantine Empire, had its capital at Constantinople. The Christian church also split along these lines. The Catholic Church became centered in Rome and the Orthodox Church in Constantinople.

● Seljuk architecture still stands today in some parts of Turkey.

Around the 11th century, Seljuk **nomads** from Central Asia invaded Asia Minor. They spoke a language similar to modern-day Turkish. Most of the Seljuk people were Muslim, followers of the religion called Islam. The Orthodox Church was afraid that the nomads would take control of Constantinople. Orthodox leaders asked the Catholic Church for help. Rome sent armies of soldiers called crusaders. Instead of helping the Orthodox Christians, the crusaders took over Constantinople themselves. The Byzantine people did not regain control until 1261.

For centuries, Christians and Muslims continued to fight. In the 14th century, a Muslim leader named Osman formed a powerful army. His followers were called Ottomans. The Ottoman military conquered Constantinople in 1453. Under their control, the city became known for education and religious freedom. Jewish, Christian, and Muslim people lived together in peace for many years.

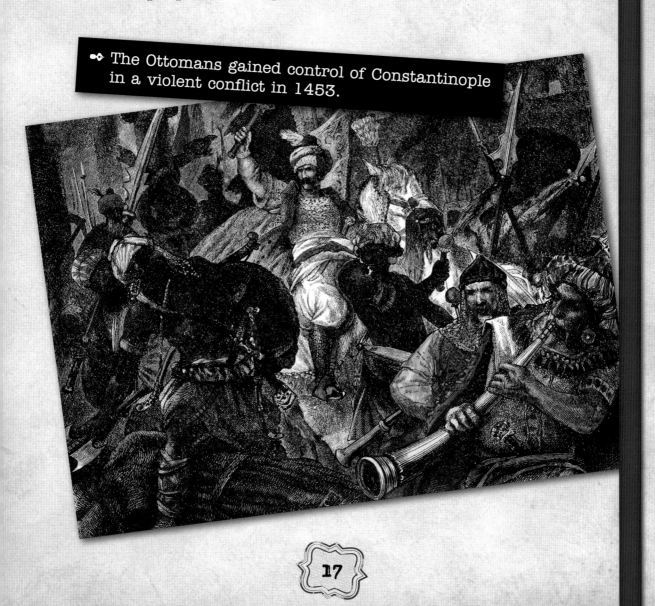

The Ottomans gained control of Constantinople in a violent conflict in 1453.

During World War I (1914–1918), the Ottoman Empire joined the Central powers, alongside Austria-Hungary, Germany, and Bulgaria. When the Central powers lost the war, the Ottomans were forced to sign a treaty that took away much of their land.

One man did not accept this treaty: Mustafa Kemal. He led Turkish troops in a fight against European forces controlling the region. The battle lasted four long years, but in the end Turkey was a free country.

➥ Mustafa Kemal (in lighter uniform) and his men fought for Turkey's independence.

☛ After winning Turkey's independence, Mustafa Kemal became the new nation's first president.

Mustafa Kemal became known as Atatürk, or "father of Turks." Atatürk thought it was important that Turkey become **secular**, so laws would not be influenced by religion. He gave women the right to vote, and he adopted the European calendar. He also replaced the Arabic alphabet used by the Ottomans with the Latin alphabet, which is the alphabet this book is written in! He moved Turkey's capital east to Ankara and changed the name of Constantinople to Istanbul.

Since Atatürk's time, Turkey has been one of the few **democracies** in the Muslim world. The military has taken over the country three times since 1960, but Turkey has always returned to civilian, or nonmilitary, rule.

Today, Turkey has two leaders: the president and the prime minister. The president serves a five-year term and can be reelected once. Since 2007, the president has been elected directly by the people. The president can recommend laws and suggest changes to the country's

To many people in Turkey, a head scarf is a symbol of faith. Muslim women traditionally cover their hair and heads. Turkey works hard to keep religion from affecting its government. One example was a law forbidding women to wear head scarves in public buildings such as government offices. In 2010, this law was removed. Some people are happy to have the freedom. Others worry that Turkey will not be able to keep religion out of politics.

↔ Tansu Çiller is one of the most important female politicians in Turkish history.

constitution. The president also appoints Turkey's prime minister, who is head of the government. Turkey's first female prime minister was Tansu Çiller, who served from 1993 to 1996.

The Grand National Assembly is the legislative branch of government. This branch makes the country's laws. There are 550 members of the assembly. Members are elected by popular vote and serve four years.

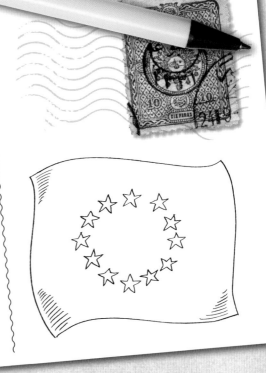

The European Union, or EU, was created in 1993. Residents of EU countries can live and travel freely within the EU's 27 member countries. Turkey has been working to join the EU since 2005. As of 2012, it has not been successful. Some countries argue that Turkey is Asian, not European. Others say that Turkey has too many financial problems or has violated human rights.

The prime minister nominates the Council of Ministers. The president officially appoints them. These ministers are in charge of different departments of the government, just like the U.S. cabinet members.

The judicial branch of government interprets Turkey's laws. This branch runs the court system, which tries criminals and helps settle legal disputes.

THE PEOPLE OF TURKEY

➥ Turkey is home to people from a wide range of cultural backgrounds.

People from many parts of the world have made Turkey their home over the centuries. As a result, its population is very diverse.

One thing that most Turkish people do have in common is their faith. More than 99 percent of Turkey's people practice Islam. Most are Sunni Muslim, which is the most common branch of Islam. Other branches include Shiite, Alevi, and Sufi.

The official language of Turkey is Turkish. Turkish is used in schools and for business. Some people may also speak Kurdish or Arabic.

Have you ever heard of a whirling dervish? Dervish is the Persian word for "monk," a person who is part of a religious group. Dervishes belong to a sect of Sunni Islam. They perform a spinning prayer called a sema. During the sema, dervishes spin with one hand held up toward heaven and God. Their long white robes twirl as they spin. Dervishes sometimes spin for hours. They believe this connects them to God.

Around three-fourths of the people in Turkey are Turkish. The country is also home to Kurds, who make up about 20 percent of the population. Some Kurds feel the Turkish government has taken away their rights. For years, they could not speak Kurdish in public or learn it in school. There were no Kurdish TV or radio stations. Some Kurds would prefer to have their own country. These arguments sometimes erupt in violence.

About 70 percent of Turkey's population lives in cities. Many people live in modern houses or apartments. Their homes have the same appliances and electronics that you might find in a house in the United States. People generally travel around the city by bus, train, or *dolmus*, a shared taxi.

●◆ Nomads do not have permanent homes.

Some Turkish people are nomads. They move from place to place, often living in tents. Nomads may rely on a herd of sheep or goats to make a living. Other people work on farms and live in homes made from mud-baked bricks.

School is required for all children ages 6 to 14, but not everyone attends. Schools are free, but there are still book and uniform fees that some people cannot afford.

Many children must also help support their families, which leaves little time for school.

Boys are more likely to go to school than girls, especially if a family cannot afford to educate all of its children. Some families believe the Qur'an, the holy book of Islam, teaches that girls should not be educated. The Turkish government is working to convince more parents to send their daughters to school.

❧ Turkish students are sometimes required to wear uniforms to school.

TURKISH

Although the Turkish language uses the same alphabet as English, the words are very different. Try saying these common Turkish phrases.

ENGLISH	TURKISH
Hello	Merhaba (MEHR-hah-bah)
Good-bye	Allahaismarladik (ah-LAHS-mahr-lah-duhk)
Please	Lütfen (LEWT-fehn)
Yes/No	Evet/Hayir (eh-VEHT/HAHR-yuhr)
Friend	Arkadas (Ar-Kah-DAHSH)
Thanks	Tesekkürler (teh-sheh-Kewr-LEHR)

Turkey has two types of high schools. General high schools prepare students to attend a university. Technical schools prepare students for a specific job. For instance, someone who wants to be an electrician or plumber might go to a technical school. Students who want to attend a university take an entrance exam after high school. This test is very hard. Many people do not get the scores they need to be accepted into the universities and programs they want to attend.

Family is extremely important in Turkey. Children often live with their parents until they are married or go to college. Multiple generations typically live in one home. Many families follow very traditional roles. The husband is the head of the household. Girls and women take care of everything around the home.

❖ Turkish children, parents, and grandparents often live together in the same home.

CHAPTER FOUR

CELEBRATIONS

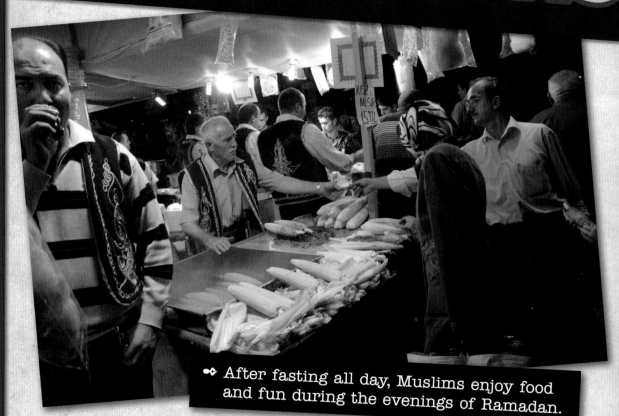

◦• After fasting all day, Muslims enjoy food and fun during the evenings of Ramadan.

Many Turkish people pride themselves on being good hosts. It's no surprise that Turkey is a country that knows how to celebrate!

One of the most important religious events of the year is Ramadan. During this monthlong fast, most adults do not eat or drink between sunrise and sunset. They feast at the end of each day.

Ramadan remembers when the Prophet Muhammad first received the Qur'an from the angel Gabriel. Many Muslims give the money they save by fasting to people in need.

Holidays in Turkey fall into two categories: religious celebrations, and holidays that observe a government event.

New Year's Day	January 1
National Sovereignty and Children's Day	April 23
Commemoration of Atatürk, Youth and Sports Day	May 19
Victory Day	August 30
Republic Day	October 29
Ramadan	Varies
Kurban Bayrami	Varies

Ramadan occurs in the ninth month in the Muslim calendar. Its dates on the European calendar are different each year. This is because the European calendar is about 11 days longer than the Muslim calendar. Ramadan ends with a three-day feast called Eid al-Fitr or eker Bayrami, the "sugar holiday." Children receive money and treats. Muslims gather in mosques to pray.

◆▸ Turkish children look forward to receiving treats and money during Eid al-Fitr.

⟶ Turkish people take great pride in their country.

The year's biggest religious holiday is called Kurban Bayrami in Turkey. Elsewhere people call it Eid al-Adha. The holiday celebrates the religious story of Abraham and his obedience to God. An animal is sacrificed during this celebration. The meat is shared among friends, family, and the poor.

Many of Turkey's national holidays have to do with the country's independence. April 23 is National Sovereignty and Children's Day. This is the day Turkey set up its Grand National Assembly. The Turkish flag is raised. Children go door to door asking for candy, similar to Halloween!

➨ Victory Day is celebrated with parades, historical reenactments, and other patriotic activities.

May 19 is Youth and Sports Day, but it's also the Commemoration of Atatürk. This holiday remembers the day Turkey's war for independence began.

Victory Day on August 30 is similar to the Fourth of July and Memorial Day in the United States. Victory Day celebrates the end of the war for independence. It also honors those who died for Turkey's freedom.

When Turkish people are not celebrating a holiday, they are enjoying sports. Football, or soccer, is a favorite. Turks also enjoy grease wrestling. Players cover themselves in slippery oil. This makes it difficult for their opponents to catch them!

The Topkapi Palace is an astonishing building. Today, the palace is a museum. It was originally home to Ottoman sultans, or rulers, for roughly 400 years until 1856. The buildings and grounds included living quarters, courtyards, private baths, stables, offices, and gardens. The buildings covered 7.5 million square feet (696,773 sq m). In comparison, the average home in the United States is less than 2,500 square feet (232 sq m)!

MAKE A MOSAIC TURKISH TILE

Turkish artists are famous for their beautiful ceramic tiles. Many can be found in mosques and museums. You can make your own version of this centuries-old artwork. It's easy to do but requires some patience!

MATERIALS

- Ruler
- Pencil
- Piece of paper
- Heavy paper plate
- Glue
- Toothpicks
- Small beads in assorted colors
- Hole punch
- Ribbon
- Scissors

INSTRUCTIONS

1. Use your ruler and pencil to draw 4-by-4-inch (10-by-10-centimeter) squares on your piece of paper.
2. Use these squares to experiment with ideas for a design.

Because you'll fill in your design with beads, it's best to use simple shapes. Geometric patterns like circles, triangles, and squares are good choices.

3. When you have a design you like, draw a 4-by-4-inch (10-by-10-cm) square in the middle of your paper plate. Copy your design onto this square with your pencil.

4. Squirt a bit of glue on one section of your drawing. Use a toothpick to spread the glue evenly across the whole design.

5. Gently stick beads into the glue. It's a good idea to place the beads around the outline of a shape first and then fill in the middle area. Put the beads close together so that each section has nice sharp edges.

6. When you've filled in your design, let your tile dry overnight.

7. Once the glue has dried completely, punch a hole in the top of your paper plate with the hole punch. Thread a piece of ribbon through the hole, hang up your tile, and enjoy!

CHAPTER FIVE

TIME TO EAT!

⚓ Turkish bazaars offer an incredible selection of spices, foods, and other goods for sale.

Walk through Turkey's street bazaars and you'll find mouthwatering kebabs, or meat and vegetables grilled on sticks. You'll also see abundant fruits and vegetables as well as some of the world's strongest coffees and teas.

Turkey's foods celebrate the country's mix of cultures. Some foods, such as kebabs and yogurt, were

popular with nomads. The warm western part of Turkey is perfect for growing olives, and olive oil is a cooking staple. It is also common to use a variety of spices when cooking. This might have been how people living in hot desert areas kept their food from spoiling.

In Turkey's mild climate, you can get delicious fresh fruits and vegetables almost any time of year. Street markets sell food straight from the farm. Because Turkey is surrounded by water on three sides, seafood and fish are common menu items.

Farmers' markets are a great place to find fresh produce in Turkey.

Turkish delight is a favorite Turkish sweet. Legend has it that a sultan wanted to make his many wives happy and asked his **confectioner** to create a special treat. Turkish delight, or lokum, was the result. It is made of sugar, flavorings, nuts, and dried fruits. It is all held together with a jellylike substance and coated in sugar. Turkish delight comes in flavors such as rose, lemon, and mint.

Breakfast in Turkey is often served buffet style. Common items include bread served with honey, butter, jam, cheese, and olives. Sometimes a hard-boiled egg or an omelet rounds out the meal.

Lunch and dinner often include soup and pilaf, a dish made with rice and vegetables. Meat is usually served ground up and mixed with vegetables. Beef and chicken are common choices, but pork is never on the menu.

This is because most Turkish people are Muslim, and pork is forbidden in this faith.

Fruit is either eaten fresh or served with meat. Yogurt is also popular, but it's not typically served with fruit as it is in the United States. Instead, it is used in savory dishes and treated more like a cheese. No meal would be complete without bread, such as a round, flat pita, or *pide*.

•➛ Pita is often stuffed with meat and vegetables or dipped in a variety of tasty sauces.

Evening meals often begin with meze, or appetizers. These include olives, pickles, and hummus, a paste made of chickpeas and sesame. Dolma, which is anything that is stuffed, is another appetizer. Cooks stuff cabbage leaves, grape leaves, peppers, tomatoes, or eggplants with a mixture of olives, nuts, rice, and meat.

➡ Dolma comes in a variety of sizes and shapes.

If you are invited for a meal in Turkey, it's important to know some basic rules. Turkish food is sometimes eaten with your hands. When it is, try not to use your left hand. It is considered unclean! Be sure to try everything that you're given, to avoid hurting the cook's feelings. It is best if you eat everything on your plate. When you're done eating, put your knife and fork next to each other on your plate. This shows that you're finished.

The most well-known dessert is baklava. This flaky pastry combines layers of fine dough with honey and nuts. Pudding desserts are popular, too. Many Turkish people also enjoy a sweet soup called *asure*, which includes boiled beans.

Turkey is a fascinating country that's rich in history, tradition, and delicious food. Enjoy!

This easy salad is good any time of year. It's especially tasty with fresh ingredients from a farmers' market or your own backyard! You'll need a sharp knife for this recipe. Ask an adult to help you.

Cucumber and Tomato Salad in Yogurt Sauce

INGREDIENTS
1 large cucumber
1 medium tomato
4 green onions
3 tablespoons lemon juice
½ cup fresh mint
½ cup fresh parsley
2 cloves garlic, crushed
1 cup plain yogurt
Black pepper, to taste

EQUIPMENT
Vegetable peeler
  (for the cucumber)
Knife
Cutting board
Mixing bowl
Measuring cups and spoons

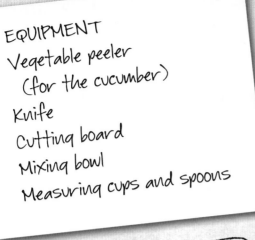

INSTRUCTIONS

1. Peel the cucumber. Ask an adult to help you chop the cucumber and the tomato into bite-size pieces.
2. Have an adult help you mince (cut into very small pieces) the green onions, mint, and parsley.
3. Mix the onions, mint, parsley, lemon juice, garlic, and yogurt together in a medium-size bowl. Season with black pepper.
4. Add the cucumbers and tomatoes. Stir gently until everything is mixed well.
5. Serve immediately, or put it in the refrigerator until you're ready to eat!

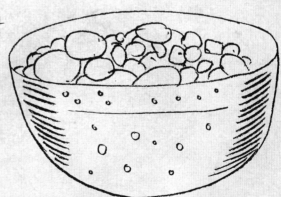

GLOSSARY

confectioner (con-FEK-shun-er) a person who makes candies and sweets

coniferous (ko-NIF-uh-ruhs) having to do with evergreen trees that produce cones

constitution (con-sti-TOO-shun) a document that sets up a government system

deciduous (di-SIJ-yoo-uhs) having to do with trees whose leaves fall off at a certain time of year

democracies (di-MOK-ruh-seez) political systems in which the people elect leaders to represent them in government

fault (FAWLT) a crack in Earth's crust

fertile (FUR-til) capable of bearing or producing vegetation or offspring

mosques (MAHSKS) Muslim places of worship

nomads (NOH-madz) people or groups who wander from place to place, with no fixed home

secular (SEK-yuh-lur) having to do with, or controlled by, the state rather than a religious body

terraces (TARE-ess-ez) a series of flat platforms, each one rising above the next

textiles (TEK-stylz) cloths or goods produced by weaving or knitting

FOR MORE INFORMATION

Books

Bowden, Rob. *Istanbul*. New York: Chelsea House Publishing, 2007.

Lilly, Alexandra. *Teens in Turkey*. Minneapolis: Compass Point Books, 2008.

Shields, Sarah. *Turkey*. Washington, DC: National Geographic, 2009.

Web Sites

Central Intelligence Agency—The World Factbook: Turkey
https://www.cia.gov/library/publications/the-world-factbook/geos/tu.html
This site is chock-full of facts and figures. It's a great way to learn more about this fascinating country!

National Geographic Kids—Turkey
kids.nationalgeographic.com/kids/places/find/turkey
Find pictures, videos, maps, and more at this fun and helpful site.

TIME for Kids—Turkey
www.timeforkids.com/destination/turkey
Visit a day in the life of a boy in Turkey or explore a guide or timeline at this educational site.

INDEX

ABOUT THE AUTHOR
Every time Vicky Franchino writes a new book about a country, she wishes that she could hop on a plane and go there! Turkey is no exception. Doesn't it sound fascinating? Vicky dreams of visiting new places from her home in Madison, Wisconsin, where she lives with her family.